From the Window
of
God's Waiting Room

A Memoir of Playful Prose and Pleasant Poetry

Bonnie Papenfuss

Table of Contents

Dedication

*This book is dedicated to the memory of my late mother,
Ida Katherine Wyatt.*

*Her love of nature, kindness of heart,
generosity and stewardship to what she believed in,
resilience in the face of life's challenges,
and trust and faith in her creator
have been my inspiration and guiding light.*

Thanks, Mom.

Acknowledgements

I want to thank all my family and friends who
have supported me in this endeavor.

Of utmost importance, my patient and encouraging husband who
spent countless hours alone while I busied myself in front
of the computer attempting to put together something
others might find worthy of a read.

Also, much gratitude to the Green Valley Writers' Critique Forum.
Without their willingness to listen and offer constructive criticism and
thoughtful assistance, the words in this book would never have
made the leap from my imagination to the printed page.

And a special thanks to Debbie O'Byrne (jetlaunch.net) for designing
my cover and assisting with all the myriad details which are an integral
part of the process leading to an actual book in hand.

Introduction

It's been many years since I first pondered the possibility of putting some of my poetry into a book. Many of my writer friends are successful authors and I've envied the fact that their words would be forever accessible in print.

Then thirteen years into my retirement, the associate pastor at our church gave a sermon titled, *What's Your Story?* His message seemed to speak directly to me. It was at that juncture my decision was made.

I invite you to enjoy these short stories and their accompanying poems in which I've attempted to share a few personal retirement experiences. Hopefully you'll see yourself in some of them. May they warm your heart with memories of times past, encourage gratitude for the present, bring a tear to your eye, and, maybe, just maybe, give rise to a chuckle or two.

As you transition between story and poem you may notice I've taken a bit of creative license in an effort to entertain and amuse.

God's Waiting Room

My husband and I retired and moved from gloomy Minnesota to sun-kissed Arizona the fall of 2004. Our new home needed a few things altered, one being the covering on our cornice boards. Red and green stripes were not at all my taste!

I embarked on a quest to our local Walmart.

The task required a whopping 15 yards of material; and, being a thrifty Midwesterner, I set a goal to find it in the dollar-a-yard bin.

Upon arrival in the dry goods department, I began wading through the haphazard mountain of fenced-in fabric. After a time, however, my hopes deflated like a balloon with a slow leak.

Then fresh excitement gripped me as I caught a glimpse of something with a background of sage green and what appeared to be leaves in the design. It held the right colors, and I loved leaves.

With renewed vigor, I unearthed that bolt from its confinement. Bingo! Exactly what I'd been looking for. Now the only question: Did the roll hold enough for my needs? I examined the end label. It indicated a remainder of 18 yards. If not for fear of embarrassment, I'd have done a jig right there in the aisle.

With a happy heart, I took my place in the queue to wait for assistance from the clerk at the cutting table. Without a doubt, she was not as excited to be doing her task as I was to have found what I needed to embark on mine.

Ten minutes passed. I reached the head of the line.

Sporting a warm smile, I said to the lackluster employee, "Fifteen yards, please."

She greeted me with a cool, indifferent stare indicating I'd best not inquire as to the pleasantness of her day.

Then a light tap, tap, tap on my shoulder and I turned to face the cloudy yet inquisitive eyes of the diminutive, white-haired granny behind me.

I will never forget the words she spoke—in such a serious tone—to me that day.

Her proclamation of God's impending reclamation gave me a turn. And though she meant it, I'm sure, as a "gentle" reminder of life's reality, it served only to provide me momentum to make every moment of my leisure years as relevant as possible.

God's Waiting Room

I'd chosen my material,
was in the cutting line.
Since newly retired,
I had all the time.

I got to the table
said, "Fifteen yards please."
New drapes were in order,
seemed like a breeze.

Then the lady behind me
snorted a query
"Do you live **here**?"
She appeared quite leery.

I turned and answered
with my friendliest smile,
"Why, yes, a month now;
just a short while."

She crinkled her brow
and pursed her lips,
then replied with authority
hands on her hips,

"That seems a big project."
then continued by stating,
"For here in Green Valley
we're all just—waiting!"

A Gift

Igot the call late November of the year we moved to Green Valley.

"So how do you like Arizona?" she asked.

"Oh, I love it here," I said. "The Sonoran Desert is so beautiful, and I feel fortunate to live where I can be out hiking or just enjoying nature every day of the year."

We chatted for a while—a casual, surface conversation, much the same as most of the infrequent chats we'd had over the years.

Until the end.

When I hung up and turned to my husband, the look on my face must have been one of panic.

"Is everything all right?" he asked.

"She's coming to visit in February."

"Who's coming?"

"My sister. And she's going to spend an entire week with us."

"Well, isn't that a good thing? Why do you look so terrified?"

I paused at his astute observation. Scared? No doubt!

Now don't misunderstand. I love my sister. However with seven years between us, we'd come of age during two very different generations. My decade witnessed bloody racial violence and the assassination of an American president, while hers saw the introduction of the original

6

microprocessor and the monumental release of *Star Wars*.

When I began business college and moved away from home, we saw each other intermittently during my visits for birthdays or holidays.

I had already finished my education, gotten my first job as a working adult, recited my wedding vows, signed for my first home mortgage, and become the mother of three little girls by the time she graduated high school.

We had never spent a week together under the same roof since she was twelve years old. What would we even have in common? I oozed apprehension.

The day arrived and we picked her up at the airport.

Almost immediately I noticed our similarities. We talked the same in voice tone, inflection, and in our choice of words and phrasing. Even our hand gestures seemed to sync.

One of our first activities included a hike in the mountains. When she emerged from the guest room that morning, we looked at each other and laughed. Each was clad in blue jeans and a chambray shirt. We resembled matching bookends.

During her stay we had so much fun together exploring, talking over mutual interests, sharing thoughts about life and love, and rediscovering a joint passion for the outdoors.

In the course of those seven days, we rekindled our relationship as children and created a very special adult bond.

As the week came to an end, I offered to do some laundry so she could return home with clean clothes. I observed, then, the most humorous likeness between us.

I handed her the pile of folded garments with a smile and said, "You know, Sis, I couldn't help but notice, we even wear the same brand and style of underwear."

"Well," she giggled, "Mom always said it was the most comfortable."

Since that first visit, she's come several more times. I do so look forward to seeing her. And during my trips to Minnesota, we always make time to be together and catch up on each other's lives.

We don't talk on the phone any more frequently, but our "connection" has certainly improved.

A Gift

Already school age when you were born.
Mom and Dad beamed—I was forlorn.

We brought you home on Christmas Day.
When asked my thoughts, I'd nothin' to say.

The folks had thought I'd be filled with love,
but you weren't a gift I thought highly of.

No longer the youngest, my life not the same.
At that moment in time, I saw you to blame.

You kept Mom so busy—not a moment for play,
and engaging with children just wasn't Dad's way.

Then I got to hold you and my jealousy was gone.
The role of big sister, I happily took on.

The months went by and you began to crawl.
I caught you at the steps before you took a fall.

Until the age of four you were something of a pest.
Admittedly, at times, an unwelcome guest.

Then playing together, time spent was fun.
Having a sister was better than having none.

After school and marriage, I moved away;
but we shared our lives at each holiday.

Then a week-long visit brought us closer.
We both shed tears when the time was over.

Sometimes the fates give just what you need;
for as years have passed, she and I both agreed

Though life took its turns and hairs faded to gray,
we've each had the other—best friends to the day.

Hunger

I'm a pragmatic, matter-of-fact, and rather non-imaginative person. I would never claim to be artistic since even the ability to draw a convincing stick person is beyond my God-given talents. And as a poet my work is neither flowery nor metaphorical, but more simplistic and straightforward.

Planning and structure are the hallmarks of my personality. I like my surroundings clean with everything in its rightful place. Any creativity I might be capable of is not going to happen if I'm surrounded by chaos.

I haven't always been like this, though. As a young person my free-spirited and unorganized nature rivaled that of my peers. If not for my mother's occasional demands to "clean up this pigsty" I could have survived my youth quite comfortably in a room amidst one giant conglomeration of clutter.

If I had to assign blame for my current condition to a particular time or event in my life it would be that of striving to be a good wife and homemaker while attempting to parent three children under five before I was the ripe old age of twenty-five.

No way could I cope without a semblance of order when motherhood itself came with such disorder. I had a schedule for each daily task and I adhered to it religiously. It's probable my "affliction" caused my daughters irreparable psychological damage.

Even in retirement this anal-retentiveness has not diminished. My husband will roll his eyes and emit a huff of derision when I insist upon cleaning the oven, scrubbing the toilets and washing the windows before leaving on an extended trip.

What if the plane crashes? I don't want our daughter opening the door to anything less than immaculate.

And whenever life leans toward the chaotic, words are my balm of sanity. Like the consoling presence of a best friend, their strength and solidity afford me great comfort. I feel nourished after creating something meaningful from a fleeting moment of emotion or inspiration.

My basic nature, however, tends to stifle spontaneity, a necessary attribute of a good author. If a dust bunny floats out from beneath the couch at the same time I'm hit with a brilliant idea for a poem, I find it difficult to ignore one to satisfy the other.

It's a constant battle. I fight it, though, because writing fills me with contentment and a sense of accomplishment—almost as much as a clean house.

Hunger

I picture them on the shelf
waiting there for me to yield;
but I've much to do
no time to indulge.
Certainly, no time to indulge.

I busy myself with housework
ignoring their beckoning.
No time for them right now;
other things come first.
Yes, other things come first.

But they haunt my thoughts,
such temptations they are;
summoning while I scrub and dust
wanting to be foremost.
Always, wanting to be foremost.

Inevitably, I succumb
to the persistent, gnawing hunger,
take up my writing tools,
and feed my soul with words.
Indeed, feed my soul with words.

Solitude

As you neared retirement, did you concern yourself with the idea you and your husband would be together 24/7?

No more would there be the freedom of motoring alone to your place of employment, sharing lunch with female coworkers, and having that precious downtime of a peaceful drive home in the evening.

Just the thought of being together within the same four walls every moment of every day could strike fear into the hearts and minds of would-be retirees.

That was not the case for me and my husband.

During the final ten years of our working careers, we lived only a couple of miles from our employer. We drove together every morning, had desks just down the hall from each other, took joint lunch breaks, and rode home side by side at close of day.

We were content spending large chunks of time together. Constant contact during retirement years would not be a problem. Or so I thought.

The truth was, though he had his golf and I had my hiking, writing, and volunteer work, I discovered—as days turned to weeks and weeks rolled into months—sometimes I simply needed solitude.

Solitude

This is my time,
my moment of
quiet contemplation.
I am not ill
nor angry, nor sullen.
I don't care to be questioned
or cajoled, or amused.

Allow me this opportunity
alone with my thoughts
to gather inner strength
and garner a peace
that comes to me
only through
quiet introspection.

For though we live
a life together,
our souls travel
separate planes;
our minds forge
divergent solutions;
and each of us needs
time for solitude
to dream, seek hope,
and gain renewal
so we might
better toil in partnership.

Final Treasure

"Hey, look at this one," I said as I kicked loose the sparkling stone from the desert dirt with the toe of my hiking boot.

Glancing over my shoulder, Sharon exclaimed, "Wow! That's a nice one!"

The rest of our troupe of Thursday morning trekkers continued walking, shaking their heads in resignation as the two of us paused to pour precious drinking water over the newfound treasure—oohing and aahing as its colors were revealed with moisture and morning sunlight.

Being experienced hikers we all knew to watch where we placed our feet, for both snakes and plant daggers. Sharon and I, however, did so with additional intent. We were rock hounds. And these our weekly treasure hunts.

Of course we'd often pause to enjoy the beautiful Sonoran Desert scenery. But the ground beneath our shoes most interested us. And if we spotted a stunning specimen nestled beneath a prickly pear, we would ignore the danger of impalement and extract it using one of our hiking poles. Yes, we had our pebble peculiarities.

One Thursday as we all gathered to decide our day's destination, Sharon's husband walked down the street to where we stood in the parking lot. He wanted to explain her absence for the last several weeks. There'd been some speculation she was on a relaxing tropical vacation, likely walking the beach and picking up anything shiny that washed ashore.

We were heartbroken, however, to learn the real reason was nothing so pleasant. Because she'd not been feeling well for a month or so, Sharon had gone for a thorough checkup. The diagnosis was an aggressive, fast-moving cancer. She'd chosen no further therapy and asked only that we keep her in our daily prayers and respect her privacy as she took her last walk down life's tenuous trail.

She died three weeks later.

She was the first friend I lost during retirement and it hurt. At the time, I didn't fully grasp her decision to refuse treatment. She was young, after all. Only in her early sixties. As years have passed, however, I've gained understanding and empathy in that regard; and I believe I would choose the same avenue should the decision befall me.

In my heart I know Sharon has found her final treasure. But I miss her. I miss our special camaraderie and shared love of all God's amazing desert creations—especially the sedimentary type.

Now when I discover a glittering gemstone on the trail I hold it up in a toast of remembrance and say, "This one's for you, my friend. This one's for you."

Final Treasure

With her I walked a footpath
traversing many a desert trail
pausing to admire a cactus bloom
or a covey of Gambel's quail.

We enjoyed a mutual love of rocks
so our gaze was at the ground
and we'd share in the excitement
when a shiny stone was found.

Then cancer struck its blow
and she chose not to fight
her suffering was mere weeks
she's gone now from my sight.

One day I'll meet my friend again
when my feet no longer roam
and I discover that final treasure
as death's trail leads me home.

No Clue

Do you sometimes pause to ponder life's great mysteries? Those things beyond scientific grasp? I mean, why can't emus walk backward? What causes the strange Taos Hum? Why do severed feet continue to wash up on the beaches in British Columbia? And my all-time favorite—why do cows, consistently across six continents, stand along the Earth's magnetic poles facing north and south whenever they're grazing or resting? Yes, it's a fact. Google it.

All those are quizzical and deserving of further research. However, there's another that is of particular puzzlement to me. Why do men find it necessary to expel surplus saliva?

Now I'm not talking about those who use chewing tobacco. That subject would need a nasty narrative all its own. I'm referring to the average male who simply enjoys engaging in the vile habit of spitting.

I don't get it. Is the moisture in their mouths different from that of their female counterparts? Is it so foul tasting or toxic that swallowing would cause discomfort or, worse yet, bodily harm? I don't think so.

Personally, I prefer my saliva stay where it's supposed to be—in my mouth. I have no need to dispense it to any location other than down my throat where, in my opinion, the good Lord intended it for disposal and recycling.

There are few things more disgusting than being greeted by and having to dodge a gross gob of spittle, its surface still bubbling, when exiting the car in a store parking lot.

Does the male of the species not comprehend how repulsive and filthy a practice this is? Does he not stop to consider the germs being traipsed from one place to another on the shoe soles of shoppers? What is the draw? Where is the pleasure in this? To quote an outmoded mantra my dear mother would often spout, "It just baffles me."

Then there are men like my sweet husband. Not the sort of person you'd expect to partake in this disturbing tendency. He has a happy and accommodating nature. Doesn't drink or spout profanities. Attends church regularly. Is gracious and kind to old ladies and children. And, for some reason, the neighborhood dogs flock for his attention. He makes his own dinner, unloads the dishwasher, and would never, ever consider leaving his dirty underwear for someone else to pick up. He's my equal when it comes to the need for regular bodily cleanliness and rivals me in tidiness around the house.

But spit? Well . . .

No Clue

It's gross, it's disgusting,
and I haven't a clue
why I have no need
and you, obviously do.

Had I known when we wed
that this was to be
I may not have been
so quick to agree.

Now we're tethered together
by vows spoken aloud
and I have no control,
though certainly not proud.

When holding your hand
down the sidewalk we stride
you pause, turn and aim
before spit and earth collide.

Peaceful Slumber

For those of a certain age, the smallest of life's pleasures can bring elation. High on my list, and yours too I'm guessing, would be waking refreshed from an uninterrupted, pain-free night's sleep.

As we age, many subjects related to bedtime are modified. We retire much earlier and have, for myriad reasons, a harder time falling asleep. And more often than not, slumber is interrupted at least once or twice during the night by the need to void one's bladder.

Even the pleasures of intimacy suffer due to physical limitations, side effects of medication, or as my doctor humorously quipped during one of my checkups, "Well, you're about as dry as the Sahara, aren't you?" (It was fortunate for her my position didn't allow for a swift kick to her shins.)

But, I digress. Let me just say a satisfying and rejuvenating sleep experience is a precious though often elusive commodity in one's golden years. And when a spouse finds a way to improve it, maybe by leaving the bedroom and relocating to a couch or lounge chair, their partner is happy to accommodate since it only adds to their own comfort.

That was the case with our friends Janis and Don, an elderly couple we met during new-member classes at our church. Like us, they hailed from the "Land of 10,000 Lakes" and the four of us became good friends.

As the two progressed into their late eighties, Don's sleep patterns changed markedly. Though true we seniors hit the sack long before the stars begin to twinkle in the night sky, Don took it to a whole different level, going to bed following the evening news. The five-thirty evening news.

Oftentimes during the night he would awake. Not wanting to disturb his wife, Don would pad out to the living room, snug himself into the corner of their cushy sectional, lay his head back, and fall sound asleep.

One morning, upon finding her husband in that familiar position, Janis went ahead with her shower, leaving him to much needed slumber. Upon her return, she found Don in the same relaxed pose. She walked past him into the kitchen and caused a bit of commotion as she started coffee to brew.

After a minute, when he showed no signs of movement, Janis went to rouse him.

He was not sleeping.

With my husband having serious heart issues,
I wondered whether I might find myself in Janis' shoes one day.
How would I cope?
It was something I needed to write about,
but a frightening scenario to dwell on.
Consequently, you'll notice I took a more humorous tone for poem's ending.

Peaceful Slumber

A crimson dawn wakes the desert
as I gaze on his motionless form
seeming restful in sleep.
Could he be dreaming?

I sip my steaming coffee
keeping him in my sight
watching with trepidation.
Did I imagine movement?

Scarlet Cardinals are chirping
mating melodies of springtime.
I can't help but ponder,
Does he hear them too?

As he lie there, so very still,
a cool morning breeze
gently caresses my cheek
seeming to ask, Isn't it time?

I knew this day would come,
nature will have its way;
regardless, still a jolt
and I wonder, Why today?

Reluctantly, I make the call
explaining there is no rush
no need for blaring sirens.
She inquires, "You ok, Ma'am?"

I assure her of my welfare
with a quavering voice
revealing false confidence
as I plead, "How long?"

They arrive minutes later
the typical determined duo
serious in their quest
young one asks, "Where is he?"

I point toward his location
keeping a safe distance
as they begin the dance
and I inquire, "Where will you take him?"

The tall one—plank prison and nifty nabber in hand—
plucks him from peaceful, coiled slumber
as he assures, "Only across the arroyo, Ma'am.
Enjoy the beautiful day, now."

A Little Hair

Certain elements of particular events in one's life are seared into memory. The weather on your wedding day. How many hours of agonizing labor you endured before the birth of your first child. In which looking glass you happened to be primping the morning you discovered your first chin hair.

Did that last one surprise you? Sure did me.

I remember the sobering details. It was seven-thirty on a Monday in June, five years into retirement. The morning sunlight from the bedroom window shined in on our bathroom mirror.

I'd just finished applying facial moisturizer when I noticed what I thought to be a piece of thread on the edge of my jaw. I attempted to brush it away, but it continued to cling. I leaned in close to grab it with my finger tips. Only then did I realize: It was not a thread. Au contraire! It was an elongated hair. A peach fuzz gone awry. A mutant. Needless to say, I was horrified.

Instead of losing hair, which I had assumed more the norm in old age, my body had now begun to sprout it in places it had no right to be. How long had it been there? Why hadn't my female cohorts, always good about the whole lettuce-in-your-teeth thing, alerted me? Did it pop out overnight? I thought back to Sunday morning service. Had my friends stared at me in a peculiar way? When we went for breakfast afterward, had they finished their meals or left them uneaten, sickened by the sight of my facial anomaly?

I had no time to dwell on it, however, since my volunteer job began at eight o'clock. So I plucked the little sucker and gave my face a cursory exam for any additional rogue hairs.

When I arrived at my desk, I wanted to broach the subject with my much-older coworker, but I didn't know how. Though she and I had grown close over the years, such a sensitive topic required diplomacy.

It wasn't like I could jump into a conversation with, "How many long facial hairs do you typically find in a week? Do you tweeze 'em, shave 'em, bleach 'em?"

Finally, though, I found the courage to inquire.

After we stopped giggling like a couple of mindless middle-schoolers, she shared a few additional unattractive and much more consequential things about getting older.

"I assure you," she said, "chin hair will be the least of your concerns."

A Little Hair

Oh no!
Can't be.
What do I see?
What DO I see!

The peach fuzz
- once oh-so-fine
has morphed into spikes
along my jaw line.

It's not possible;
I'm only 60.
Please give me back
my face at 50!

Old age has crept in.
Thought I'd never get there.
So many maladies.
Seems so unfair.

But as Mother would say,
"Life isn't fair."
And in the whole scheme,
it's just a little hair.

"Joy" of Christmas

In early December of 2009, we were getting ready for a visit from my oldest daughter and her family. They were coming from snow-covered Minnesota to the sepia-colored desert to share the holidays with us. It was an exciting time.

Outside, we'd already hung yards and yards of store-bought icicles from the eves of our roof; and I was determined to cover every inside flat surface with as much glamour and greenery as time and money would allow.

While draping the fireplace with intertwined pine-scented garland and twinkling, multi-colored mini lights, my mind wandered back to the past. To the years as a young mother of three when my prime focus was to fashion a winter wonderland that would put a sparkle in the eyes of my cherubs on Christmas morning.

Do you remember those days of shopping, baking, wrapping, and decorating? I'm sure you can recall the stress involved. As moms, we wanted everything to be perfect for our little ones. And since we bore the majority responsibility for success or failure, sometimes, amid the chaos, what we yearned for most was a half hour of uninterrupted "me" time in the warmth of a relaxing bath.

During the early years of my first marriage, my husband and I lived only a mile from his parents who would insist upon joining us for our holiday festivities.

I felt the need for everything to be flawless for my "exemplary" in-laws. They were wonderful grandparents who doted upon our little girls; but somehow, regardless of my best efforts, they always managed to make me feel inadequate.

As I attached the final piece of greenery to the mantel that day, I knew one thing for certain. My joy from the anticipation of our daughter's visit was the complete opposite of the trepidation of so many long-ago Christmas mornings.

"Joy" of Christmas

Bangles and bells
Garland and glitter
Cookies and carols
I'm in such a twitter

Can it all come together?
Will I make my deadline?
It's just 'round the corner
'n' I'm not feelin' so fine

The tree's a-tilting backward
My cookies they're burnt crisp
The presents aren't wrapped yet
And this drat headache persists.

I hustle to finish the baking
Clean the sink and polish the drain
Things just have to be perfect
But I fear I'm going insane.

The time finally arrives
I await the doorbell
Instead, the phone rings
A sad tale to tell

The flu's hit them hard
Barely able to speak
Flat on their backs
Wanting only to sleep

They send their regrets
But my eyes are dry
I say, "I'm so sorry."
Glad they can't see me lie.

A Mother's Bliss

"Hi, Mom," she said. "I called to give you and Dad some exciting news."

"Well, hang on a second. I'll put you on speaker."

"Hey, Little One."

"Hi, Dad."

"Your mother says you have something important to tell us. So what's going on?"

"Well, we've decided to make it official. We're getting married."

Living so far from family during retirement is challenging, especially, I believe, for mothers. Whatever the situation, whether bad news or cause for celebration, I'd prefer to be there in person to help and console or partake in the rejoicing, though that's not often possible. My dear husband, in most cases, is content to listen from afar.

So, as it's been for the past fifteen years, each time the phone rings, we never know whether we'll be sharing in someone's delight or be left with aching hearts and a sense of helplessness.

With this announcement, we were thrilled.

"That's wonderful honey. Congratulations," we said, almost in unison.

"Thanks. We're very excited."

"So when's the big day?"

"We've chosen the 4th of February."

"Oh, that's wonderful. We'll start looking for air flights. We have a three-week tour overseas scheduled during that time, but with trip insurance we can cancel and choose a later date. So, no problem."

"Mom, slow down. Please, don't go changing any plans."

"Well, of course we will, honey. There's no way we're going to miss your wedding!"

"Mom, I'm trying to tell you, it's ok. We've decided to have a very private ceremony aboard a cruise ship. It will be just the two of us. No friends. No family.

"So you see, you don't need to rearrange your schedule, but I would like your motherly advice about a few important items."

A fleeting image of our beautiful daughter standing at the altar surrounded by her friends and loving family dissolved before my mind's eye.

"Of course, dear," I said, after a second's pause. "I'd be delighted to help in any way I can."

As she chattered on I dabbed at a tear, thankful it couldn't be seen over the telephone.

A Mother's Bliss

She's involved me in the details
via computer and telephone
we've chosen the dress and flowers
with music to set the tone.

She'll wear a designer gown
and Mendelssohn will play
her hands will cradle red roses
while I'm a Date Line away.

The Captain will officiate
a privilege he's endowed;
they'll each exchange a ring of gold
and recite their sacred vows.

I'm sad that I'll not be there
What mother wouldn't be!
but a private ceremony is their choice
for this coupling on the sea.

Yes, they'll be cruising toward Hawaii
as I journey to the "land down under"
but my bliss is believing their life together
will be brimming with love and wonder.

False Courage

"**N**ow step your feet, one at a time, through these loops," he instructed. "I'm almost ready to attach the canopy. There's a slight breeze today. Perfect weather. We should have about a ten-minute ride."

There I stood, buckled and belted into a tandem safety harness. As a woman in her sixties, I should have been thrilled to have a handsome, young Frenchman strapped to my backside. Instead, my turbulent tummy threatened to unload that morning's complimentary breakfast. I was about to walk off a mountain.

How in blue blazes did this happen?

Early the previous morning, my husband and I had completed a two-week tour of Australia and had boarded a plane for New Zealand—our next destination.

As the aircraft descended into Queenstown, we were struck by the beauty below. The lush vegetation filled the thirsty eyes of us desert dwellers.

After checking in to the hotel, our guide took the group on a walking tour of town. I attempted to listen but the scent of new-mown grass and the vista of the Southern Alps casting shadows on the calm, crystal water of Lake Wakatipu distracted me.

Then my husband nudged me to glance upward.

High above us gliders floated off the mountaintops, their bright, rainbow-hued sails creating a kaleidoscope of color like nothing I'd ever witnessed. We stood, transfixed by the sight.

My dear spouse then turned to me and said, "Well, if someone were foolish enough to consider doing something like that, I can't imagine a more beautiful place in which to have the experience."

Back at the hotel we unpacked, dressed for the evening meal, and headed to the bar to join others of our group for a drink before dinner. We'd all enjoyed a couple of libations, when one of the more adventuresome members of our troupe strolled in. She wore a wide grin and waved a marketing flyer from the hotel kiosk.

With infectious enthusiasm she announced her decision to go paragliding the next day. After checking out the company's history and safety record, our guide had assured her of its stellar reputation and reliability.

My God! This woman intends to jump off a mountain, trusting her life to a stranger sporting an elliptical piece of rip-stop nylon.

Everyone shared in the awe of her bravery. High-fives circulated all 'round. Then we enjoyed another beverage while she and our esteemed leader went from couple to couple with the sign-up sheet, attempting to recruit others.

When the commitment form reached our table, my ultra-conservative hubby (at the time, slightly tipsy) turned to me and asked, "You want to give it a shot?"

To be honest, I assumed he was joking. But feeling more plucky than sane, I replied, "Sure. Why not!"

Then with a sly wink of his eye and a boldness I'd not witnessed in all our years of marriage, he affixed his signature. Without hesitation he slid the paper to me.

What to do? I was not letting him go by himself.

By the time we'd sat down to dinner, eight foolhardy thrill-seekers had added their names to the list. Our guide was dumbstruck. She'd taken many groups on this tour during her decade of leadership. Never had any of the participants chosen this.

In the morning, after a few sobering cups of coffee, we gathered at the excursion office to sign the necessary hold-harmless agreements. Then, each in turn, we stepped on the scale. Our weight in kilos was marked in grease pen on the backs of our hands.

Good grief! What if the scale is off today? Mine at home can easily fluctuate by ten pounds. Will I be too heavy? Will we drop from the atmosphere like two ducks full of buckshot?

I had no time to ponder, however, as the base attendant gave some final instructions and cautioned us regarding the three-part expedition— the last being a climb to the summit over a damp forest trail covered in pine needles.

He warned once we began the journey up, there would be no turning back. The singular way down was to jump.

An hour later, having survived a halting funicular ride, a seesaw jaunt on an aging ski lift, and a grueling quarter-mile hike, my husband and I, as the first of our illustrious octad, summited the mountain.

And there we stood, harnessed to our appropriately-weighted comrades. Mine indicated he and I would fly first.

Looking over my shoulder, I mouthed what I thought certain to be my final "I Love You" to my partner of more than twenty-five years.

We stepped onto the artificial turf extending over the edge of the cliff. I could feel my heart beating. My saliva stuck in my throat.

I'm expected to step off a mountain!

Pacing in unison, we moved forward two steps. Back two. The sail filled. Then forward again as our feet lifted from the ground and we floated into the sky.

False Courage

He steadies me–
this partner I do not know.
As I step through the loops,
he buckles and ties
and tightens the straps just so.

Then he lays out the chute
all straight and tangle-free,
attaches the lines,
hooks his harness to mine,
and checks the flag for a breeze.

These mountains are so high
and my heart's in a race.
He assures, "Don't be afraid,
I do this all day."
So I put on my best brave face.

We walk two steps forward
wind catches the chute
we float off the mountain
gliding free like the swallows
treetops below and a sky so blue.

He positions the camera for video
to capture this memorable event
then coaxes, "Relax now, let go;
flap your arms like a bird,
for we'll soon be on our descent."

The time passes so quickly
and he's piloting down.
We land ever-so-gently
as if we'd rehearsed
and I stand: both feet on the ground.

It was thrilling and I feel so courageous;
but I just can't help but recall
it was due to peer pressure
before last night's dinner
and an excess of alcohol!

An October Walk

What was I supposed to say when my husband informed me one day early in our retirement planning of his desire to relocate somewhere in the desert Southwest?

Well, my immediate response, which I chose to keep to myself: *You want me to live where there's nothing but sand, rocks, and cacti with prickers the size of sewing needles? I don't think so!*

Instead, what came out of my mouth was, "Well, honey, maybe we should start checking out some various locations."

Like many folks, I envisioned the desert—any desert—to be a barren, dusty landscape with nothing visually interesting.

Then he brought me to this verdant valley and I fell in love. We'd both found our nirvana.

His idea of an idyllic retirement was being able to chase a small, dimpled ball around on the grass for hours at a time several days a week. And, in the company of a bunch of like-minded fellas, he did just that for more than a decade.

My happiness derived from my surroundings. I joined a hiking group, and every Thursday morning we'd head out for parts yet unexplored.

Through the tutelage of two experienced leaders, I learned the names of the native plants and trees and developed an understanding of the role each living creature played in the multi-layered ecosystem.

Those weekly journeys also afforded me the opportunity to indulge my love of words. As a budding poet, I could be hit with inspiration while contemplating the clouds or gazing at a fragile cactus flower.

Trekking the trails in this unique land of basin and range has been an experience leading to many attempts at capturing in verse the ever-changing beauty and diversity of my adopted desert home.

An October Walk

The winding, open desert trail stretches out before me, reaching for the foothills. Many feet of myriad origin have traveled this path. It feels alive with history.

The spotlight of midmorning sun illuminates the yellowing leaves on a multitude of ocotillo plants, as scarlet acacia seed pods vie for attention in the shrubbery below.

I'm startled by the frenzied beating of wings as a quail flutters from beneath a prickly pear to find shelter among the low-hanging branches of a mesquite tree.

A tiny gecko, sunning himself on a nearby rock, darts his head to and fro keeping a watchful eye, his kaleidoscopic colors shimmering in the morning light.

Hedgehog cacti, their summer growth complete, dot the parched earth. Winter rains will nourish them—their fuchsia blooms, the springtime bouquets of the desert.

My steps are halted by the rattle of another familiar inhabitant warning of its presence and reminding to be ever watchful of where I place my feet.

As I continue, my vision is captured by the movement of native grasses, their small white tassels glittering in the sun's rays as they sway with the gentle morning breezes.

The quiet of the moment is broken by the ragged call of a nearby cactus wren, and I wonder if one of the large grasshoppers around me is fated to be its next delicacy.

I pause, pluck a sprig of creosote, and rub it between my thumb and finger. Breathing deeply, I let its pungent odor remind me of the scent of the desert after a spring rain.

Clusters of tiny yellow and white flowers claim their place among the ground flora, as injurious shin dagger plants threaten to impale with one false step from the footpath.

Bare spikes of agave and yucca stand in stark silhouette; devoid now of blossoms but reminding of the magnificence and multiplicity of the desert in every season.

And, as I rest for a moment in a rare spot of shade, I'm greeted by the buzz of a bee gathering nectar from a mallow flower as I ponder the grandeur of this wondrous place.

Lessons Relearned

"Oh honey, I'm so sorry," I said, as our daughter poured out her heart. As a single parent she worked sixty hours a week while raising a confused and lonesome teenage daughter. A storm waiting to blow in. That day had arrived. My granddaughter had made some poor choices.

During our mostly-one-sided conversation, I felt sad and helpless. I wanted to reach through the phone and envelop her in a loving, reassuring hug.

Having gone through those parenting years myself with an in-law who freely offered her "expert" opinions, I had learned long ago the folly of giving unsolicited advice to grown children.

So I took it all in and kept silent.

But as my daughter talked on, I thought to myself: *I just might be able to help without giving any motherly counsel.*

So, ignoring all the warning bells in my head, I offered, "If you like, I'll fly to Minnesota and stay for a while. I could be company for her and help for you around the house."

I caught her off guard. After a short pause, she replied, "Well, that's very generous of you, Mom. I'll think about it and let you know, ok?"

"Of course, honey. Just give a jingle whenever."

For the next two weeks, I waited and fretted. Had I said the wrong thing? Caused her additional distress?

Finally, I got the call.

With a tender voice she said, "Mom, I appreciate your offer, and I love you for it. But I can't reward my daughter for bad behavior. Your coming would do just that."

I had been gently reminded of my role in the familial framework.

Since that conversation of several years ago, our granddaughter has grown into a smart, confident and caring young woman—mirroring many of the same admirable traits of her mother.

And, to be sure, this grandmother's gone back to just listening.

Lessons Relearned

I didn't mean to meddle
on that very unhappy day.
Sometimes it's just hard,
knowing what's right to say.

I'm aware it can be trying,
mothering the teenage years.
I just wanted to assist you;
and be close to dry your tears.

Though many miles divide us,
my thoughts are there with you.
For regardless of the distance
a mother's love stays true.

Often it's tough to be silent
but the lesson relearned is clear.
My charge is to simply listen
and say only, "I love you, dear."

Something About Nothing

"What time do you want to leave tomorrow?" he asked.

"Well," I said, "if we head out at our usual seven o'clock, we should get there about two-thirty in the afternoon. Given the time difference, we might be able to check in at the hotel."

"Do you want to make our customary stop in Wickenburg for brunch, or would you prefer to eat sooner?"

"I'm good with that," I said, "as long as you swing through McDonald's on our way out of town for my senior coffee."

That's how our typical conversation would go the morning before heading out for our yearly, week-long January gambling jaunt to Laughlin, Nevada. With its more subdued, slow-moving pace (much like us), this mecca on the Colorado River had long ago superseded Las Vegas as our favorite place to play.

The drive from our retirement suburb south of Tucson takes about seven hours, allowing ample time for bathroom breaks and a food stop. My husband and I share the driving.

My normal "assignment" is from Wickenburg—known as the Dude Ranch Capital of Arizona—to the quaint little town of Wikieup, lacking any fame whatsoever. Once or twice (and only if my hubby's released his death grip on the arm rest and fallen asleep), I've managed to retain my position behind the wheel all the way to Kingman.

Arizona's #93 is a section of highway with scenic rolling hills, colorful river valleys, and an abundance of stately saguaro. Following a portion of the road aptly named Joshua Tree Parkway (a vast landscape of the giants of the Yucca family), the desert floor becomes curiously littered with rocks. Big rocks. Rocks with no obvious sign of origin.

Then, as one approaches the tall, weathered sign for the village of Nothing—a truck-stop ghost town with an intriguing tale all its own—you see them: magnificent mounded monoliths. A roadside attraction like none other.

Something about Nothing

They say it's Nothing
one might agree
past the Joshuas
on U.S. 93.

On the road between cowboys and kings
at mile marker 1, 4, 8
rests the ghost town of Nothing
amid the saguaro landscape.

It began in 1977
a sign, a store
a fuel stop for truckers
population: 4

No election for mayor
Les Payne was just there
greeting his constituents
from a tattered brown chair.

Les lived in his camper
out back of the store
had Nothing to brag of
wanted nothing more.

Destroyed and abandoned
fire's left only the sign
that's all that's in Nothing
weathered with time.

You may think from these words
the legend is the allure
but alas it's the backdrop
in this place so obscure.

A sight so celestial
nothing else can compare
standing in grandeur
their splendor I'll share

Massive pyramids of behemoth boulders
reaching toward the clouds
How I wish those mounds of rock
could speak their creation aloud.

So let them say it's Nothing
but I'll have to disagree
Nothing has something special
left by nature for all to see.

Come Back

One spring day, I was trekking a mountain trail I'd never before explored. It was a beautiful, clear day in late March and the weather was beginning to warm. The soft, still air was pungent with the pleasant scent of damp earth and creosote, remnants of a late-season overnight mist.

Above me gleamed a brilliant azure sky dotted by cotton-ball clouds. Alongside the path, stood an aging hedgehog cactus, its transient fuchsia blooms adding blush to the khaki cheeks of the desert.

I was overwhelmed by the splendor of my surroundings—a moment of true inspiration. I wanted to write about it. However, whipping out a notebook and pen would not have been judicious.

Imagine the reaction of my hiking companions if I'd hollered, "Guys, wait up. I need to sit on this rock for a while and compose a nature poem."

Nope, that would not have made me popular.

And there are other moments of revelation which can be very inopportune and detrimental to one's creativity.

Take, for example, the short interlude before one dozes off. Experts have concluded our brains are the most innovative during that brief period previous to falling asleep.

I know this is true. Some of my best ideas occur right as I'm about to nod off. It's very inconvenient. I'm tired. It's cozy under the covers. I just want to go to sleep. Certainly, I wouldn't turn on a light—interrupting my hubby's slumber serenade—just to jot down a couple of key idioms.

So whatever the circumstance, my technique in the past has been to memorize initialisms for expressive phrases such as BAS (brilliant azure sky) or CBC (cotton-ball clouds). By doing so, I'd remember them later, whether returning from a hike or waking from a nap.

With those few crucial letters, I could then recreate the words and recall the scene and my corresponding emotions with enough clarity to create a vivid verse.

This method used to work well, but no more. The old gray matter has stopped functioning as efficiently as in my younger years.

Nowadays, nothing at all comes back to me. Not a letter. Not a word. Not a clue.

Come Back

I'd been resting for just a short spell
then arose with a story to tell

Threw my covers aside, stood and then
with thoughts in my head, I raced to the den

Sat down at the computer to write
before those ideas could take flight

But that fickle brain played tricks
on my waiting finger tips

And what appeared on the screen:
not what my mind's eye had seen

Once again, I'd failed to hold on
and the words—were just gone

Now, it's oh such a pity
all I have's this little ditty

Just a few words that rhyme
to show for all my time

I guess I'll return to the sack
maybe my muse will come back?

Sunday Ritual

"Oh, Mom, please don't cry. I promise I'll call every week. We've already arranged an unlimited long-distance plan, so you and I will be able to talk as long as we want."

That was my pledge as we stood by the back door, her arms wrapped tightly 'round me, the two of us sharing a rare embrace.

It was the day before we planned to pack up our Minnesota residence and head to Arizona. Because of my husband's heart condition, we'd taken early retirement and were looking forward to spending our leisure years in the warmth of the desert sun.

That day we'd driven an hour north from our place in the suburbs of St. Paul to say goodbye to my mom who lived alone in the family home nestled in the woods of Elk River. To be truthful, I hadn't thought Mother would miss me that much, given our life-long contentious relationship; however, her tearful reaction said otherwise and I was deeply touched.

I'm a middle child, you see. Growing up I was easy-going, cooperative, and, unfortunately, the one upon whom my mother found it most convenient to level her disappointments and frustrations. I loved and respected my mother, and I know she loved me; but some days she could do nothing but find fault.

So even in retirement, as a woman in my mid-fifties with grand-children of my own, talking to my mother on the phone had the potential for unpleasantness. That aside, I remained faithful to my promise; and every Sunday I would pause, take a few deep breaths, and dial the phone for our weekly chat. Some topics I knew to be safer than others. With that in mind, I'd attempt to guide the direction of the conversation. On occasion, I would avoid censure altogether.

And I never protested her verbal attacks. Well, once. It happened during an extended visit to Minnesota. I had decided—against my better judgement—to stay with Mom. I planned to help around the yard, assist in the garden she was so proud of, and just share quality time together.

At breakfast one morning, two long weeks into my stay, she found it necessary to criticize my "unhealthy" food choices. Her harsh words wounded me and I shot back an unkind response.

She looked at me with eyes that failed to hide the hurt and said, "Well, I guess you told me, didn't you? I hope you feel better."

I didn't. And I never did it again.

Eventually Mom moved from her home in the country to an assisted living facility and, two years later, to memory care. I still made my Sunday afternoon calls and was delighted when she recognized my voice and greeted me by name. I knew those days were fleeting. And during her final year, my joy was made greater yet since our weekly conversations tended to be pleasant and free of conflict.

Two of our children lived close to Mom and would visit with weekly regularity. Early on she would recognize them. But the mind is a strange thing. As time passed, Mother's memory took her back a few decades, and visits from my girls could elicit a darker-than-desired response.

I'd laugh through my tears when my middle daughter, who looked and sounded most like me, would call and announce, "Well, Mom, I was you again today. I'm really sorry Grandma has disrespected you all these years. When I visited this morning all she could do was scold and find fault, and it made me sad."

Of course, I felt empathy for my daughter, but, I admit, it was mixed with a sense of validation.

And every Sunday I'd pick up the phone and dial, hoping the voice on the other end would answer with cheerful recognition.

Sunday Ritual

I ponder momentarily,
close the bedroom door,
turn on the overhead,
punch in the numbers,
and wait:
eight rings, nine.
A weak voice answers.
Mine rises in volume.
She greets me by name.
We talk for a time.
A pleasant chat,
no unkind words.
Her day's activities
told over and over.
She grows weary.
We say our goodbyes
punctuated with
I love you's.
I give thanks,
and wonder silently:
How many more
Sunday rituals
before my voice
is that of a stranger?

I Understand Now

"What a surreal experience," I told her. "We stood near the base of Ayers Rock, something I'd only dreamed of seeing in person, and watched the sunset bathe that sandstone monolith in shades of crimson and gold."

"That's wonderful," Mother replied. "I'm so happy you've been exploring the world. But don't forget about the many amazing natural wonders in this country."

That was part of the conversation on a day in February of 2013. My husband and I had just returned from a tour of Australia, New Zealand, and Fiji. It had been an awesome trip and I was excited to share the adventure.

I knew, however, exactly what Mom referred to with her comment. Anyone did who'd ever spent time talking to my mother.

Accompanied by a couple of close friends (my father preferred the comforts of home) Mom had traveled extensively, both in this country and abroad since the time we kids had become adults with lives of our own.

Regardless where she'd been or what she'd done, the conversations would always wind back around to her enchantment with the Rocky Mountains.

She'd once said to me, "Standing in the shadow of those majestic peaks is where I feel most connected to my creator."

It was her place of tranquility. Where she'd often gone for "refueling." A site of restfulness and renewal.

A few years after my dad's death in 2002, mother's declining health grounded her from further wanderings. But by that time, my husband and I had retired and begun our own travel adventures; and Mom delighted in hearing of our exploits around the world.

But regardless the context of our phone conversations—as was the case this day—she would often slip in a comment about her place of personal paradise. I knew she wanted me to experience it. To share that with her. But it was not to be.

In the pre-dawn hours of Sunday, February 14, 2016, my mother's heart stopped beating. Though small consolation, we were told she passed peacefully.

That May we decided instead of flying to Minnesota for our yearly visit with family, we would go by way of an extended driving vacation, allowing the freedom to see parts of the United States we had not yet explored.

Our journey took us through a large portion of the Rocky Mountain range from its namesake national park up through the Grand Tetons and Yellowstone.

As I stood gazing at those awe-inspiring pinnacles, I felt a pang of regret. Then a reassuring perception as if Mom were standing right next to me.

I could almost hear her whisper, "See, isn't it amazing?"

Bonnie Papenfuss

I Understand Now

She'd traveled here often over the decades
to this Rocky range that bisects the West
extolling its splendors to any listening ear.

Jagged, ebony, snowcapped peaks
jutting heavenward, spearing ivory clouds
skirted by lime aspen and emerald pine.

As my eyes feast on the breathtaking majesty
I feel the warmth of Mother's joyful smile
in the heat of the morning sun on my back.

Her breath floats on the breeze that carries
the sweet aroma of evergreen to my senses
as I inhale, deeply, the cool, fresh spring air.

Before, I had only listened.
But, now—now, I understand.

My Hero

"Well, Ida," he said. "I have good news and bad. The good news is, we got it all. The bad news—I forgot to reconstruct your belly button."

Mom loved to tell that story when anyone would inquire about her surgery. It tended to lighten the mood and it kept folks from asking too many other personal questions.

She would explain with her usual wry wit how she'd smiled at the apprehensive physician and simply stated, "Well, I don't think wearing a bikini is in my future anyway, Doc, so we won't sweat the small stuff."

I was a junior in high school when my mother heard the dreaded "C" word. I knew nothing about breast cancer or any type for that matter. Mom had glaucoma and had used drops in her eyes for years. She'd also suffered through the healing process of a compound fracture of the wrist, but nothing so life altering as a dire disease.

In the mid-'60s lumpectomy procedures were not yet common practice. Her doctor recommended a radical mastectomy. After surgery, she was minus her right breast and had an incision from the upper arm pit down through her navel. And without a lot of rehab options available at the time, she administered her own physical therapy at home.

My mother viewed the human condition through a streak-free window of optimism and determination. For her the glass was always half full, and rarely did she shy away from a challenge. If Mom made up her mind to do something, it got done.

I think she regarded cancer as just one more test of her resolve. She tackled it with the tenacity of an injured athlete determined to complete the race. And she did, living a relevant life with sincerity and hopefulness.

Showing the way until the age of 92.

My Hero

No pink ribbons to adorn in the '60s
But a scar that diagonally transects her body
Puckered — armpit to navel
The doctor said, "We got it all"
But, who really knows
Five years, the magic number
Make it and you're free
An unkindly-long prison sentence
No hope of acquittal

She snugs her toes to the baseboard
Poised for home therapy
An arm mutilated by the surgeon's scalpel
Hangs weak and unwieldy
Reluctant for another day's journey

There's tension in the air
As her fingers touch smooth paint
Embarking on their upward sojourn
Creeping, inch by inch

Tears begin at shoulder height
Streaming down her flushed cheeks
The pain, agonizing
The only sound,
A soft moan of determination

* * * * * * * *

I'd watched with youthful fear and concern
But so proud of her strength of spirit
Her bravery has been my life's inspiration
Her positivity my resilience in adversity
She was my hero in a sleeveless housedress

One More

"**M**a'am, are you all right?"

"Yes," I said. "I'm fine. Thank you for your concern."

I knew the clerk. She'd worked at Walgreens for years. With an uncanny ability to calm the crankiest of senior citizens, I'd watched her conquer many a conundrum. Yet, passing through aisle two on her way back to the register, she held the look of someone unsure how to deal with the customer standing before the array of bedazzled Mother's Day cards, weeping quietly.

I'd spotted the perfect one, you see.

Mom loved all of nature, but birds held a special place in her heart. The cover featured a stunning male cardinal. A scarlet beacon set against a backdrop of indigo and emerald.

Standing there, debating the purchase, my mind wandered back over the decades.

I remembered my childhood days when part of the excitement of any holiday was crafting a creation of my own imagination, usually with such an abundance of glitter it took until the next special occasion to vacuum up the remnants.

Mom, with tears of joy, was happy to get it and happier yet it pleased me to have made it for her.

As a teen, I rejected the idea of a hand-made card believing it a childish endeavor. Dad would drive me to the local five-and-dime, hand me a dollar and leave me to my own devices and a hundred choices. It proved a daunting task and not one at which I excelled.

I remember one year when Mom read with delight my scrawled "Happy Mother's Day" greeting on the envelope only to discover a get-well wish inside. In my defense it did have pretty flowers.

And, as one would expect, she stood it with her others in a place of honor on the china hutch.

Then I got my first job. I felt much more mature and so proud. I had my own money to spend on something special just for my mother. And at that age I always took time to write a few heartfelt phrases below the printed prose.

Mom loved that part the best.

After marriage, my life became a whirlwind of activity. Occasionally I'd lament the time it took from my harried schedule to drive to the store and choose the perfect commercialized words of endearment.

Sometimes the task would remain undone for so long all I had to offer my dear mother was a dogeared generic note card dug from the back of the drawer—a few words of gratefulness and affection written hurriedly on a page otherwise devoid of fancy verse.

She cherished it, nonetheless.

During retirement, with days of long-awaited leisure filled with social engagements and travel, her only gift, on many a holiday, was my voice over the telephone.

She relished all our conversations, regardless the day or occasion. And since I've now reached that sensitive stage myself (when one realizes you're too old to be of relevance to anyone younger than sixty), I look back with greater understanding, empathy, and a bit of sadness.

I know she would have appreciated my calls to be more frequent.

As I stood there in the aisle, reminiscing, intent on the display, the heartbreak of earlier spring events washed over me.

I slid the colorful card back into its appropriate slot. Tears of remembrance moistened my cheeks.

All I wanted that day at that moment was one more opportunity, for no special reason, to call and hear the joy in her voice.

One more occasion to pick the perfect greeting.

One more chance to express my forever love and gratitude.

One More

So simple when I was small
no shopping, no money at all
globs of glitter on glue
cut hearts, one or two
no need for a trip to the mall.

As a teen I was oh so lazy
picking one just made me crazy
mushy words of affection
I had no direction
grabbed a cover of bright yellow daisies.

Years later with kids of my own
a husband, a job, and a home
I'd race to the store
five minutes, no more
seal, stamp—in the mailbox I'd thrown.

Then retirement, and so many plans
just a postcard from some far-off land
had I been so inclined
to chat more on the line
I mightn't now be so maudlin.

For it's May and the day is near
I gaze at the shelves, wipe a tear
an orphan I am
so like a lost lamb
If only I had one more year.

A Mid-Summer Affair

Retirement began with much excitement for the future. Our calendar filled with dinner invitations, cultural events, tee times, and travel plans. There were days so penciled in with options choosing became difficult.

Nowadays, however, it seems those small, numbered squares lack space to accommodate the multitude of doctor appointments, test procedures, and surgeries. I say that with a modicum of tongue-in-cheek, but also a good bit of truth.

Growing old is not for sissies. Joints wear out. Hair (what little we retain) loses all pigment. Arthritis sets in. Eyes cloud over. One's bladder is no longer an ally.

As my wise mother often said, "Getting old was sort of fun, but being here is hell."

And sometime between the festivities of your last working day and the point at which you realize you've become a hard-of-hearing, white-haired, slow-moving senior citizen causing a traffic jam in the grocery aisle, something quieter but no less sinister has been taking place.

I'm referring to the changes in the delicate covering we all took for granted in our youth as we slathered on the baby oil hoping to acquire the coveted, beach-bum tan.

First you notice a dry patch or two. You buy a special lotion. Then a couple of "age" spots. No big deal, get out the concealer.

Next, seemingly out of nowhere, a few of those pesky keratoses appear. Often referred to as senile warts (nice name, right?), they're rough and ugly but not especially menacing. The doctor simply whips out a torch-like object, resembling something from a ghost busters movie, and "freezes" them with liquid nitrogen. They puss. They scab. They fall off. You're left with just one more scar on your long-ago flawless complexion.

Then it happens. Well, it did to me anyway.

During the skin scrutiny of a yearly physical my doctor paused to proclaim, "Hmm, this is a questionable spot indeed." *Questionable? Just what does that mean?* But, without further explanation, she referred me to a dermatologist. A male dermatologist.

Being an obedient patient, I made the appointment, but I had no clue what to expect. I was certainly not prepared for half-pint nurse Nancy's demands to strip to my bootie socks, don the ever-so-attractive paper wrapper, and take my place on the exam table. After all, we were talking about a tiny red spot—on my forehead nonetheless!

So there I sat, a wrinkled, saggy-skinned, fleshy woman in her sixties who'd been seen by only female doctors since the birth of her last child. To say I was anxious would be a gross understatement.

Then the door opened. He stood there before me. My breath caught in my chest.

A Mid-Summer Affair

My heart is beating rapidly
and my palms are clammy.
I hear him in the next room
his voice gentle, reassuring.

I try to relax, then close my eyes
picturing his imposing stature
a body, muscular and nimble
his complexion fair and flawless.

It's been six long months
since our last rendezvous.
Snuggled under the light cover
my skin turns to gooseflesh

as I recall the sensation
of his smooth, gentle hands
and serious, sapphire eyes
exploring every inch of my body.

The door latch breaks my trance
as he strides into the room
and flashes that brilliant smile
disarming and seductive.

This was difficult the first time
not knowing his expectations
but I'm more comfortable now
as he approaches with intent.

I wonder what he's thinking
as he scans my nakedness
from the tip of my tiniest toe
to the top of my freckled forehead.

Finally, when he's finished with me
he steps back, smiles and says,
"All looks good. Wear your sunscreen
and I'll see you again in January."

Though the verse implies otherwise, that embarrassing
first experience caused me to search out a female dermatologist.
I'm sure my adonis was a good physician—
just not the right one for this old lady.

It's All About Her Smile

On Thursday afternoons I'm a regular participant at a writers' critique forum.

Members read from their original works and receive constructive criticism from each attendee. All genre are represented.

My usual contributions consist of book reviews for the local newspaper and an occasional poem. I'm always pleased when my work kindles the emotions of my fellow writers.

At one meeting, I read the poem titled "It's All About Her Smile."

As comments went 'round the table, one member paused to wipe her eyes before sharing her thoughts.

"Bonnie, I'm so sorry," she said. "I knew you were still adjusting to your mother's passing, but I had no idea you were burdened with a sibling's illness also."

Well, truth be told, I wasn't.

My sister, seven years younger than I, was in perfect health. I had written the verse for a variety of reasons, none related to my sister.

Naming her had simply given me a vehicle with which to express my emotions.

The actual impetus for the poem had come from a variety of experiences including my mother's last years suffering with dementia and the often heartbreaking visits to elderly friends spending their final days in memory care units.

Many of the group thought the poem moving and relatable. They encouraged me to submit it to the annual writing contest of the Society of Southwestern Authors, which, after much deliberation, I did.

To my amazement, the piece won top award in the poetry category that year.

It was the first time I felt like a "real" poet.

It's All About Her Smile

Last year,
we'd go shopping every Saturday
have lunch at our favorite cafe
discuss our individual plans for the week
share stories and laugh together
and when we'd part, she'd smile and say,
"We're so lucky to have each other.
I love you, Sis."

This year,
I shop for all her basic necessities
eat lunch at a corner table for one
as I plan my weekly schedule of visits.
When together, I tell stories and she laughs
and when we part, she'll smile and say,
"I'm sorry I don't remember your name,
but it's so kind of you to stop by."

A Better Way

For many years my mother's oldest brother lived on the property adjacent to my folks. After serving in WWII, he became a reclusive bachelor who preferred the solitude of the woods to the company of others.

But his kindness and generosity earned him my deepest affection as an uncle. When he passed away in 1986, most of his siblings and their adult children gathered at my parents' place to help with the necessary arrangements.

Having no input to those discussions, two of my older male cousins walked through the woods to clear out Uncle's run-down cabin.

He'd been a hunter so guns held the biggest draw.

But when the "treasure seekers" returned, in addition to the bounty slung over their shoulders, they both wore an uncharacteristic look of childhood mischief.

Bringing his hand from behind his back and holding it out to me, one of them said, "Hey, Bonnie. We found this in Uncle's shack. Do you know what it is?"

"Well, it looks a bit like some sort of a pipe; but it's such a strange shape and Uncle didn't smoke."

After their ruckus laughter subsided, they informed me it was a marijuana bong. I'd never heard of nor seen such a thing. Yes, I was thirty-seven at the time but far from worldly.

Horrified, I asked, "You mean all these years I had a pot head for an uncle?"

"No, silly. It was his medicine of choice. There's a patch of it growing out back of the cabin. He had glaucoma just like your mom and my dad. You know it runs in the family, right?"

Yes, that part I knew, though obviously I lacked in the complete knowledge of treatment options. I was, however, keenly acquainted with the familial affliction.

I'd witnessed my mother putting drops in her eyes several times a day since my first year in junior high. They were expensive, came in a tiny, hard-to-grasp bottle, and stung upon application. She did not like them.

Mom wore glasses which made it difficult, both with and without, to see where to hold the bottle in order for the drop to fall in her eye versus down her cheek.

I always felt sorry for her. Destiny demanded she continue the ordeal for the rest of her life.

But Mother took it in stride and never complained. For her sight to be saved, it was the best way—then.

A Better Way

Since my youth I'd watched her
Knew it likely was my fate
Yet when told in my late sixties
The news still hard to take

Doctor said "No worries;
I'll laser a tiny hole
Giving you extra drainage
Less pressure is the goal."

Surgery took but a moment
A warm tingle's all I felt
In an hour I saw clearly
My remedy'd been dealt

No plants to harvest and cure
Nor drops three times every day
If Mom and Uncle were with us still
I think they'd choose this better way

All That Matters

My husband has a memory like a bull elephant on steroids. For all things sports-related, that is.

If asked, he could quickly conjure up the teams and score of the 1999 Super Bowl, tell you the winning quarterback, and announce which player received the coveted title of MVP.

FYI, the Broncos won 35 - 19 over the Falcons and the quarterback was John Elway in addition to being named the game's most valuable player. And, as an aside, Elway proclaimed it his last game before retirement.

Ok, so you didn't want to know all that any more than I did, but it is what it is.

And I'm not just talking football. Oh no! Regardless the sport, he could tell you the minutest statistic—such as weather conditions—about any game making it into the record books in addition to those less significant, whether golf, basketball, hockey, baseball, or bowling. Well, probably not that last one, but you get where I'm going.

And though all this may be a bit of an exaggeration, there is one fact you can take as the gospel truth. You would not want to play any sort of sports trivia game with my husband. You would lose. He would win. Hands down. Every time.

But although his memory banks may be almost filled to capacity with irrelevant sporting facts and figures, he's reserved a small nodule of gray matter for something very important: his wife.

Like most loving and devoted husbands, whenever he looks at me his mind's eye recollects the slim, attractive young woman he married. The one with the freckled nose, flawless skin, and hair the color of a midnight sky. The girl who stood on the altar and promised to honor and cherish till death do us part.

He recalls all the experiences we've had and the love shared as we've walked life's path together.

I'm so very thankful for that.

And if he does, by chance, notice a few wrinkles and folds, he remembers: it's smarter not to mention them.

All That Matters

Late in the darkness of the evening
I slide silently beneath the covers;
but slumber eludes me
as my thoughts go 'round and 'round
with the rotating of the overhead fan.
I ponder my reflection of moments ago –
deep-set wrinkles, sagging jowls, countless age spots –
and I mourn the loss of the once taught, smooth-skinned body
age has remodeled into this framework of folds and furrows.
Then the rustling of sheets and I feel his warmth
as he moves close and drapes an arm over my shoulder.
His soft, warm breath caresses my neck
and I know: this is all that really matters
as he whispers, "I love you, beautiful lady."

Pay Attention

Remember being a newlywed and having any trivial dribble coming out of your mouth taken in with rapt attention by your new life partner? Well, let me ask you this: Is your better half still a good listener? Does he mute the TV and make eye contact when you speak?

In my humble opinion, familiarity and gender-related hearing impairment complicate the information-sharing paradigm.

Often, when I attempt to impart my thoughts on a topic of concern, my dear hubby of more than thirty years has a tendency to half listen, and that's only if it's commercial time.

Now, for sure, I love my husband. He's the best thing that ever came into my life. However, when it comes to conversing about matters of unease, he reacts as the typical man. If there's a solution, fix it. Otherwise, let it go. Move on.

Women don't share to seek resolution. We do it for the camaraderie of a caring, sympathetic ear. Someone to listen and pay attention. Acknowledge our anxiety.

I don't blame the male population for this deficiency. We're simply created differently. And, to be fair, just as we suffer their lack of solicitude, they bear our female passion.

As I get closer to entering my eighth decade, one thing causing me great trepidation is the thought of being afflicted by and dying from some long-affecting, debilitating disease.

Living in a senior citizen community of all ages, I've had to watch several of my friends leave this earth. The departure is seldom swift. More often it's after months or even years of unpleasant, sickening, life-altering treatments.

Many times, after I've visited a friend who is wasting away in some staff-deficient facility, its halls permeated by the not-so-scintillating scent of Eau de Urine, I just want to pour out my overwhelming sadness and terror. It's a situation I pray neither of us is forced to inflict upon the other.

But when I broach the subject with my husband, his customary response is, "Well, it's likely. I guess we'll cross that bridge when we come to it."

I get that. But it doesn't help. Usually I can't hold back the curtain of tears, so I seek washroom solitude.

After a thorough eye cleansing, I pull myself together, call a girlfriend, and make a lunch date.

We talk about our ailments, sadness over losing friends, and mutual angst for what the future might hold.

And we depart with laundered hearts.

Pay Attention

Am I invisible?
My voice not audible?
Is no one paying attention!

This life on earth
so tenuous, so fleeting;
illness strikes, disease ravages.
My fear of death is palpable.

Sit with me, my friend;
hear me, take my hand,
share with me your solace
and—pay attention.

Rewards

Senior citizens love to feel privileged as a result of our longevity on this planet. After all, we've raised our families and, in so doing, endured more than a half century of disappointments and difficult times.

Yes, our dues have been paid. It's nice to get some recognition for that, right?

I remember my delight the first time a TSA agent, standing stoically at airport security, said to me, "Ma'am, you don't need to remove your shoes. Just place your belongings on the belt and proceed through the scanner."

Wow! I applaud members of the think tank who came up with that one.

Another perk I particularly enjoy is getting a senior coffee for under a buck at the local fast-food drive-thru.

And if it happens to be a Monday and the caffeine gets me pumped for a shopping trip, I head for my favorite clothing store and browse for hours, happy knowing I'm going to save 15% on my total purchase.

Age has its advantages in other aspects as well.

There's the lifetime pass into national parks; discounts on cell phone plans, rental cars, and cruises; cheaper movie tickets; smaller, less-expensive menu options; and designated days of the month when those of the white-haired generation are entitled to 10% off at the local pharmacy or grocery store.

All those money-saving options are great, but what we pensioners prefer is getting something, anything for free.

Rewards

Precious little papers
oblong or square
punched or initialed
a single X is rare

Cut from the ads
picked from the holder
gathered and stacked
like neat little soldiers

They're here somewhere
wrapped in a band
I'll search every pocket
to find them if I can

I try the back zipper
then fish out the pack
I fiddle with the binder
in a hurry to unwrap

She's coming straight toward me
white paper on her tray
there's no time to waste
she'll want me to pay

I hand it over graciously
she sees it needs no punch
It's got all that is required
and today I get free lunch

Life's Compass

My mother was a smart lady. She and I, however, didn't always see eye to eye. In fact, conversations with her could sometimes make me want to push the mute button and pour myself a glass of chardonnay. (see Sunday Ritual)

Though we had our differences, I valued her wise counsel and tried, in most instances, to implement the suggestions she might have for a particular conundrum.

Like the events of April 1979, when my world turned upside down.

My then husband had failed the task of building up business for a new branch office. His company's three-year time allotment had come to an end.

They planned to move us back to the bustle of the Twin Cities from the slow-paced northern Minnesota town my family and I had grown to love.

We had the option of remaining there, of course, but my husband would need to find other employment.

He wanted to relocate. I did not.

In a phone conversation with my mom about this distressing dilemma, she gave me the most sensible advice which has stuck with me throughout life's tribulations.

She wisely stated, "Well, Bonnie, things could be a lot worse. Be thankful for what you have, dear. And think of it this way: It's Easter. A season of hope. A time of new beginnings."

Her sage words calmed me and instilled a renewed sense of optimism. I stopped lamenting my losses and attempted instead to concentrate on my blessings.

And each time the universe has seen fit to fling metaphorical manure my way, I've closed my eyes and listened to her voice. A simple statement of a long-ago spring morning. An affirmation that's continued to give me direction and comfort throughout my life.

I miss my mother. I even miss our sparring.

But I'll always have her love in my heart and her maternal morsels of wisdom etched in my memory.

Life's Compass

I need to call
to talk with you
nothing important
just idle chitchat
to share the day
our thoughts
  opinions
    emotions.

I want to listen
to hear your voice
across the line
words of knowledge
my life's compass
to sooth
  reassure
    guide.

I grab the phone
then remember
and my heart aches
with fresh emptiness
for, I cannot call
to talk
  listen
    share.

Small Victories

Have you had your annual Medicare "wellness" checkup this year? The name is such a misnomer, don't you think? And if by chance you are feeling well when you go in, it's likely you'll be left questioning your future physical condition upon departure.

I'm referring to all those inane questions they insist upon asking.

My doctor had the gall to inquire, "Have you had any problems with leakage?"

"Not yet," I said, "since I'm pretty sure you aren't referring to the recent patching of our roof."

She wasn't amused.

Did she think me candid enough to admit I'd been at the drug store last week perusing the sizing chart on the adult diaper packages? Nope, not something I intended to share.

Next she queried, "Have you experienced any feelings of depression?"

"No," I said. "but I imagine the whole bladder leakage thing will bring 'em on."

After a glare of impatience and some vigorous keyboard strokes, she spouted another embarrassing inquiry, "Are you sexually active?"

I felt certain she wasn't alluding to what I kept in the drawer of my bedside table; so I simply answered, "Well, not as often as I'd like."

I visualized smoke coming out her ears. No gold star for me.

Then the familiar finale to our little powwow. I was prepared for this.

"Earlier, I told you three words to remember," she stated with an air of superiority. "Can you repeat them back to me?"

"Sure," I said. "Head, mouth, spoon."

"Hmm, that's correct."

Her voice held a detectable tone of disappointment. I'm sure she hoped to delete me from her patient roster by justifying a referral to an Alzheimer's specialist. But I fooled her.

Little did she know I'd been able to recall those words only by creating a mental image of the Valley-girl "gag-me" phrase of the '80s which fit well with my current mood.

Yes, I had, once again, tricked her into thinking my memory remained excellent.

The reality was something different.

Small Victories

I lower my legs and coach old bones from my comfy recliner.
Bare feet pad softly on cool tile as I head toward the kitchen.
Passing through the archway, I pause to ponder my purpose
as my eyes scan the surroundings for clues.

Dinner is over. The dishwasher's run.
I'm not hungry. I'm certainly not thirsty.
Then, as I turn—defeated—to leave,
my ears catch a slight crackling sound.

Eureka!

I stride with purpose to the recycle bin,
drop the contents from my hand
and return—victorious—to my recliner.

A Patch

"Hello, it's nice to meet you. Are you just visiting the area?"

"No, we rented a place here for three months."

"Where are you from?"

"We live in northern Wisconsin, and you?"

"Well, we're originally from Minnesota. But we've been here full-time for almost fifteen years now."

That's just a snippet of the conversation one might expect to have when meeting a new friend in this retirement community.

It could be someone waiting patiently behind you at the grocery store, the unfamiliar folks sitting next to you in church, or your new neighbors stopping on the sidewalk to chat before proceeding with their Chihuahua's morning constitutional.

Regardless the situation, the dialog would continue with questions back and forth about children, grandchildren, and activity preferences, usually concluding with an invitation to get together over drinks and munchies.

Because my husband and I retired in our fifties, we began our leisure years as the youngest at most social engagements. But it didn't matter. Age seemed irrelevant. And through our involvement in various pastimes, we made friends of all generations.

But as we aged so did our older companions. Soon the downside of living in a retirement community became clear as couples lost mates and "players" in each of our activities began to cycle.

The process of losing a spouse, whether from injury, disease, dementia, or simply loss of interest, has been painful to witness and heartbreaking for loved ones left behind with only faith and fond memories.

A Patch

the splendor of a summer desert sunset
the ugliness of a relentless, incurable disease

the wail of sirens down a quiet city street
the peaceful aura that washed over him

the clamor of a telephone with kind condolences
the silence of their bedroom at day's end

the loss of a life partner, so playful and loving
the presence of an emptiness unique in its scope

the healing that comes of grief time with loved ones
the heartbreak of looking toward a life alone

the utterance of comfort words–sincere, yet pointless
the bizarre quiet of a rubber-on-asphalt parade

the gaping parched ground of his final resting place
the salty dampness of tears down her cheek

the faith that sustained them giving her solace
the certainty of grace, a patch for her heart

Your Loss

During a portion of my career, I worked in a building which also housed the school district's senior citizen center.

Older folks from the surrounding area would come daily to play cards, swap stories, make crafts to sell in the gift shop, and enjoy a low-cost, healthy lunch.

As employees, we also had access to the cafeteria. The typical low-salt menu choices didn't interest my palate in the least, but on occasion I'd order a salad.

Upon exiting the kitchen, bowl in hand, I would often pause for a moment, eavesdropping on the fascinating discussions of those who'd come to enjoy their noon meal with friends.

One day I bravely asked to join a table. After sharing looks of obvious surprise, they welcomed me with the utmost hospitality.

I listened as they told incredible tales of WWII, hardships of the Great Depression, retirement travels around the globe, lost loves, and loves reunited.

The delight in my attentiveness showed on their faces. It was like watching a bouquet of withering flowers return to full bloom.

After that, I joined them with regularity, picking a different table each time. They not only gave of their knowledge and experience, but also answered my questions without judgement or prejudice.

Sharing with them was an honor, and I look back on those instances with a sense of privilege.

Nowadays, as a senior citizen myself and having been enlightened several times to the younger, more-mobile generation's apparent disregard, I can say with authority that it's distressing to feel ignored or invisible due solely to the number of years showing on one's face.

Please don't think me angry. I'm not. Ageism is a fact of life, continuing from generation to generation. It's something we think little about until we ourselves are of an age to be affected.

It's frustrating, however, to feel irrelevant. We've lived a long time. We know things. We have much to contribute.

Your Loss

Why don't you see me?
Why don't you listen to me?
Why don't you value me?

You see only with your eyes –
your focus on my slow gait,
and the multitude of creases in my face.

When I speak,
you turn to others for conversation
believing my opinions

to be antiquated and irrelevant.
You attach no significance
to my years of experience

and little merit
to the storehouse of knowledge
I could share with you.

One day you'll walk in my shoes
and you will look back with shame
and a sense of loss

that you bumped by me in haste,
ignored my words of insight,
and dismissed me as simply: old

Millie Mae

For vacations during our working years, if we weren't feeding the Vegas slots, my husband and I would often opt for a relaxing cruise.

We mostly floated the Caribbean because of its warm temperatures during Minnesota's winter season when the "chill" tended to freeze the snot in your nose with one step out the door.

And after having explored many of the little islands, all touting the same tourist trappings, we preferred to spend the majority of our time enjoying the myriad activities available on-board.

Following a bountiful breakfast buffet, you could find us relaxing on a comfy, cushioned poolside lounge chair, cooling off with an iced latte while enjoying a good read.

On those rare occasions when the sun took unkind refuge behind a thunderhead, we might sit through an old movie in the ship's theatre or, as a last resort, head for the game room for a round of bingo or horse racing with those of the more average cruising age.

After the evening meal, we'd move into the auditorium for the night's live show. Since included in the cost of the voyage and always worthy of an audience, we seldom missed a performance.

Later in the evening, my hubby and I would take advantage of another entertainment option. Yup, you guessed it, the casino. And if lady luck saw fit to grace us, we might be feeling perky enough to show off our moves in the disco.

Ok, that never happened. But the opportunity existed.

I must confess, however, to our ultimate favorite activity at sea—the art auctions. With a festive atmosphere and free mimosas, why would we not? And if we over-imbibed just enough to cloud our common sense, we could be caught doling out some serious coin.

Over the years we accumulated several of a particular artist's hand-watercolored lithographs. Since retirement, a couple have gone the way of the local thrift store, but we still have a few gracing the walls of our home.

A favorite titled "The Vintage Years of Millie Mae" has always hung on my side of the bed.

Until a few years ago, I would gaze each morning at her aging hull, beached on the shore, and feel a bit of wistful nostalgia—an inquisitive wonderment of possible long-past escapades.

Nowadays, however, she's simply cause for painful pause.

Millie Mae

There was an aura about her
she wouldn't be ignored
speaking past adventures
begging to be restored.

She was unique and quirky
I bid from the floor
others raised paddles
but I made the score.

A small wooden houseboat
she was beached on the shore
her hull cracked and peeling
a farmer's faded yard decor.

Chickens pecked 'round her
dogs dozed on her floors
her frame rotted with years
and each season's downpours.

Upon waking, I'd smile
as I pondered her lore
but lately my outlook's
not so curious anymore.

For she shows my past with clarity
those more relevant days of yore
as "Millie" foretells my future
a tale I'd prefer to ignore.

It Escapes Me

While browsing with intent through a rack of ladies blouses at the local thrift store recently, I paused to glance up. A warm smile of recognition on the face of the lady opposite the aisle greeted me.

Without hesitation, she came around to my side of the rack and enveloped me in a warm embrace.

Almost in unison we both said, "It's so good to see you."

"Yes," I said. "It's been a couple of months, right?"

"Oh, more than that I think," she stated.

"Well, how have you been?"

"A lot better than some of my friends."

"Oh, who's having trouble?"

"It's terrible," she said. "Remember Louise from Bunco? She was taking her daily walk and fell on the concrete. Broke her hip and busted her right arm in several places."

"That's awful."

"It sure is. She spent two weeks in the hospital and now she's in a rehab facility. She'll be going home soon, but I doubt she'll ever fully recuperate."

"What a shame," I said. "At our age it's tough to come back from something like that. But you're doing ok yourself?"

"As good as someone in her eighties can expect, I guess. Just the usual arthritis aches and pains. I lost my little Yorkie recently though."

"Oh, I'm so sorry. What happened?"

"Well, Ralph stuck his nose under a large agave and was bitten by a rattlesnake. I spent a good deal of money having him treated; but as old as he was, he just couldn't recover. It was very sad."

"Yes, the loss of a beloved pet leaves such a hole in your heart," I said. "You have my deepest sympathy."

"Thank you, that's very kind. Well, I'd love to hear more about what's going on in your life, but I have to cut our conversation short. My husband's condition has worsened lately and I hate to leave him home alone too long."

"I understand. Let's not wait so long to see each other again, though, ok?"

"Definitely," she said. "Give me a call. We'll do lunch."

After we hugged goodbye, I turned back to the task at hand, but my mind was churning in an attempt to conjure up her name. Let's see, I thought. She mentioned a sick husband, a Yorkie called Ralph, and indicated we have a joint friend named Louise from Bunco.

Wait. I've never played Bunco!

It Escapes Me

There was a young woman of sixty
retirement, she thought, was just nifty
then she got old
or, so she was told
for her memory went rather swiftly

The End—NOT!

Turning fifty was no big deal. I still felt as I did in my forties, so it was just a number. And since my husband and I kept busy with our jobs and planning for our leisure years, I spent little time worrying over a few lines or wrinkles.

Even at sixty, having been retired five years, I continued doing most of the physical things I did in my fifties. I didn't have the stamina I once did; but I had my health, a loving spouse, and retirement had proven as awesome as I'd imagined it would be.

When I looked in the mirror, I could see the passage of time. But I tried not to dwell on it.

Then came the year leading up to my next zero-ending birthday.

The anxiety began one day when a friend referred to the color of my hair as "a becoming shade of gunmetal gray." *Was that a compliment?*

Then one morning, raising an arm in use of my curling iron, I noticed my epidermis had—seemingly overnight—disavowed any attachment to my dermis.

Disturbing, indeed.

Next came the yearly physical. I was put through the wringer with tests. (And anyone who's experienced a mammogram knows that phrase is more than just an overused cliché.)

Following eye scans, biopsies, MRIs, x-rays, CTs, and ultra-sounds, I began regular visits to the ophthalmologist, neurologist, dermatologist, and gynecologist—culminating in a total of eight sundry surgeries covering maladies from forehead to foot.

Thanks to God's grace and the skill of surgeons, I came through it all unscathed. Except for a few scars, of course.

Experiencing the events of the past year, however, has served to illuminate the realities of my future as I embark on the journey into my eighth decade of life.

My physical abilities will change as the years go on. That's a given.

But I'm so grateful for the awesome adventures and relative good health my husband and I have enjoyed during these first fifteen years of retirement.

And though I live in a town jokingly referred to as "His" waiting room, I know God would want me to continue striving to be a good and faithful servant and live every day with grace, gratitude, and as much gusto as this old body can muster.

Because it's not over, yet!

The End—NOT!

I woke on Monday and it was gone;
gone before the light of dawn.

I couldn't find it, searched and searched.
Maybe I forgot it in the pew at church?

No, I pondered, it might just be
my houseguest took it, for it was free.

Or maybe I hid it and don't remember.
I'll likely find it come December.

But I need it now. It's important you see;
for without it I'm just not my best me.

But there's no sense to cry or wallow in sorrow.
I'll say a small prayer it appears tomorrow.

Then I'll don my PJ's and have a good read.
A restful night's sleep. That's all I need.

Morning brings clarity, but in vain you see.
For my youth, will not, be returning to me.

And though it's true, the "bloom" is gone,
I'll give God thanks for each day's dawn.

Epilogue

Thank you for reading my words.

If I were to offer any retirement advice, this would be the gist of it:

Once your place of employment is in the rearview mirror, don't waste a moment.
Do all the things you've ever dreamed of, and do them with abandon.
Be fearless. Attempt the unthinkable. Scare your grandchildren.
Make memories and take pictures (to prove you did it, of course).
Don't dwell on lines and wrinkles. Your friends pay them no heed.
Display to others a heart of compassion and you'll be thought of with fondness.
Speak often of lost loved ones. To be remembered is all one hopes for.

About the Author

Bonnie Papenfuss and her husband Larry moved from Maplewood, Minnesota to Green Valley, Arizona fifteen years ago to enjoy their leisure years in the warmth and beauty of the Sonoran Desert. Though neither was a teacher, both retired from life-long careers in the field of public education.

Today Bonnie enjoys reading, writing, traveling, exploring nature, and spending time with family and friends. She also contributes a monthly book review for publication in the local newspaper and has done so for the past seven years.

Her poetry speaks to the love of family, the perils of aging, and the beauty of God's creation. You can find samples of her work in the OASIS Journals of 2013, '14, '15, '16, and '17 in addition to several smaller anthologies.

Bonnie has been an active member of the Santa Cruz Valley Chapter of the Society of Southwestern Authors and a regular attendee of the Green Valley Writers Critique Forum for more than a decade.

She and her husband have a blended family of five grown daughters. They are the proud grandparents of six and great-grandparents of one.

You can contact her at lbpapenfuss1260@gmail.com